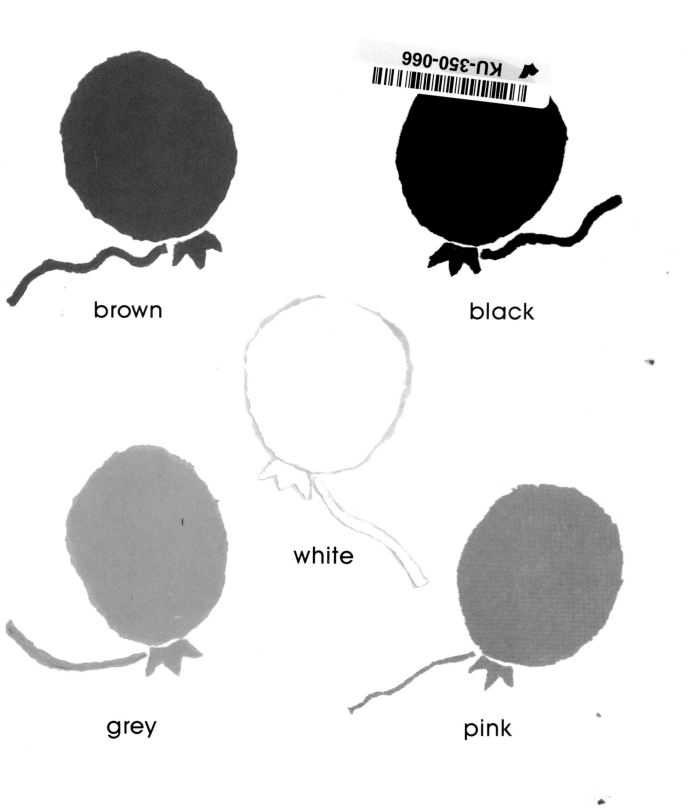

brown

black

white

grey

pink

For Simon

Educational Advisor
Lucinda Pearce

Published exclusively for
Books for Children
Whiteway Court
The Whiteway
Cirencester
Gloucester GL7 7BA
by Walker Books Ltd
87 Vauxhall Walk
London SE11 5HJ

First published 1990

Printed and bound in
Hong Kong by Imago

ISBN 0-7445-1861-X

BOOKS FOR CHILDREN

This book belongs to:

_____

_____

_____

_____

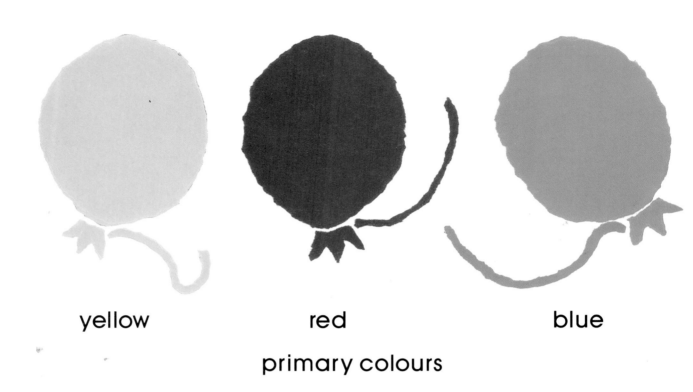

yellow   red   blue

primary colours

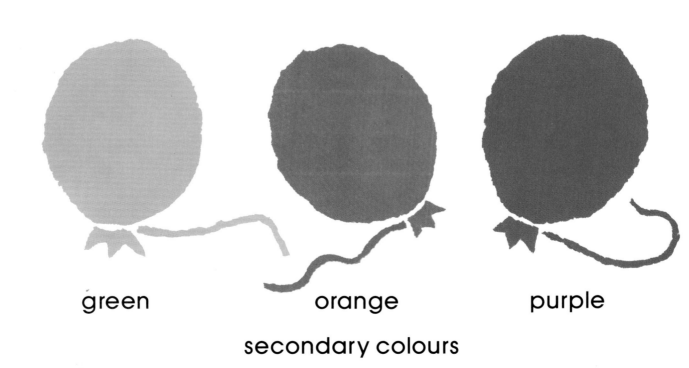

green   orange   purple

secondary colours

COLOUR PARTY

Anni Axworthy

BFC
BOOKS FOR CHILDREN

in association with

WALKER BOOKS · LONDON

yellow

red

blue

Yellow, **red** and **blue**
are the primary colours.

green

Yellow and blue make green.

orange

Red and **yellow** make **orange**.

purple

Red and **blue** make **purple**.

Green, orange and **purple**
are the secondary colours.

brown

black

white

grey

Black and **white** make **grey**.

pink

Red and white make pink.

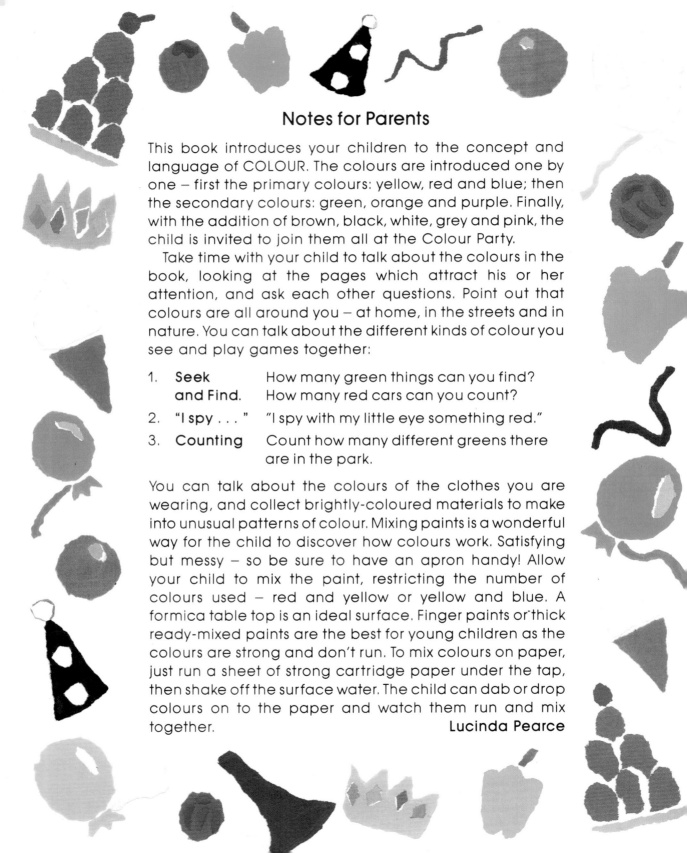

Notes for Parents

This book introduces your children to the concept and language of COLOUR. The colours are introduced one by one – first the primary colours: yellow, red and blue; then the secondary colours: green, orange and purple. Finally, with the addition of brown, black, white, grey and pink, the child is invited to join them all at the Colour Party.

Take time with your child to talk about the colours in the book, looking at the pages which attract his or her attention, and ask each other questions. Point out that colours are all around you – at home, in the streets and in nature. You can talk about the different kinds of colour you see and play games together:

1. **Seek and Find.** How many green things can you find?
   How many red cars can you count?
2. **"I spy . . . "** "I spy with my little eye something red."
3. **Counting** Count how many different greens there are in the park.

You can talk about the colours of the clothes you are wearing, and collect brightly-coloured materials to make into unusual patterns of colour. Mixing paints is a wonderful way for the child to discover how colours work. Satisfying but messy – so be sure to have an apron handy! Allow your child to mix the paint, restricting the number of colours used – red and yellow or yellow and blue. A formica table top is an ideal surface. Finger paints or thick ready-mixed paints are the best for young children as the colours are strong and don't run. To mix colours on paper, just run a sheet of strong cartridge paper under the tap, then shake off the surface water. The child can dab or drop colours on to the paper and watch them run and mix together.   **Lucinda Pearce**

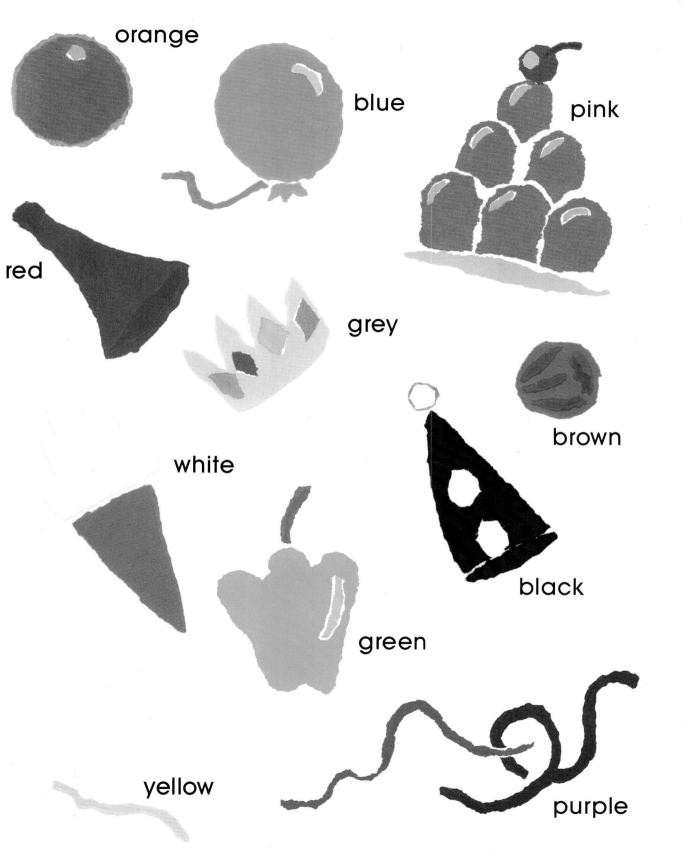

orange

blue

pink

red

grey

brown

white

black

green

yellow

purple